Praise for *Indigo Hours*

"Nancy's haiku is very powerful in its simplicity, and how it is at that tender intersection of beauty and pain. Her writing is beautiful, her experiences deeply touch your heart. Anyone living with the slide of dementia, or any other loss, will be reassured, comforted and at times uplifted by her gifted writing. A truly amazing and meaningful book."

–Deb Chisholm, MEd, CMC, BCC

"The poems are beautiful. Light, color, and emotion jump out from each verse. Nancy provides eyesight for all of us who have loved ones in need. One feels both the tangible and spiritual needs of both the lover and the loved one."

–William Geiger Jr., Pomeroy Professor at University of Vermont

"Nancy Stone's *Indigo Hours*, a collection of her haiku and scratchboard drawings, is an invaluable gift to the reader. She eloquently voices the fears, the complexity and the hope that attend her life as a caregiver. She offers perspective and possibilities with honesty and grace. This book is a great comfort no matter the challenges one faces—a lovely reminder that none of us is truly alone."

–Debra Runge, caregiver

"As the partner of a loved one with dementia, I enjoy Nancy's haiku immensely. She holds her caregiving experiences up to the prism of haiku to distill into poetry the essence of each moment along her journey with her husband. Her poetry helps me reflect on my own journey with my wife."

–Chapin Kaynor, caregiver

"Nancy didn't choose the journey her true love's brain took them on and yet she certainly has chosen to be alive to it. These haiku are snapshots of the complexity of honest moments and her full participation in the richness of the path that chose her….such wisdom and wrenching and healing and being brave enough to share them."

–Jason Imanuel, poet

"Nancy's book is a heartfelt meditation, in haiku and visual poetry, on her passage into the mysterious journey so many of us are forced to take with a loved one. Neither a recipe for healing nor a plea for understanding, she shows us a path for acceptance. Her words and art will be familiar and comforting to anyone who is embarking on a journey into the confusing darkness of dementia."

–David Yandell, Professor Emeritus of Pathology at University of Vermont

"The raw, honest emotion of caregiving is captured in these flowing words. If you are or have been a caregiver to someone living with dementia, your heart will tug and squeeze with acknowledgment and complete understanding. As someone who works in the world of dementia and lives it personally, I read these more than once and laughed, cried, sighed, asked myself 'why,' and shook my head 'yes' several times. Nancy, thank you for sharing your journey with the world in such a concise and elegant way!"

–Cathy Michaels, CPD, director of community relations at The Arbors at Shelburne

"Nancy Stone's poetry will touch your heart and remind you of the complexity and preciousness of life."

–Jane Dwinell, coauthor of Alzheimer's Canyon:
One Couple's Reflections on Living with Dementia

"It would be impossible to put into a small reflection the impact that Nancy's writing had on me. I really loved reading the progression in haiku. Amazing work! The simple rhythm of haiku invited me on a five-year journey of transformation. *Indigo Hours* beautifully captures the challenges of caregiving, the frustration of forgetting, and the flexibility required to navigate dementia. As Alzheimer's progresses, the poems encourage the reader to shift focus from the external and bold activities to turning inward and finding joy in the simple things in life — like a short haiku."

–Meg Polyte, policy director at the Vermont Chapter of the Alzheimer's Association

"*Indigo Hours*' introspective haiku and evocative art combine to take readers on a journey through the battles of letting go and holding on, loss and love, and despair and hope. We come out the other side of the journey with an increased ability to make meaning of the human condition, a reminder to take care of ourselves, and a call to cherish the moments we have with the ones we love. The work is marked by tenderness and a sincere effort to help all who might pick it up. Astounding."

–Lucas Dunn, educator

"It is my honor to help guide families through the very difficult process of choosing a new home for their loved one suffering from dementia. Every journey is unique and often heartbreaking. The artwork and haiku in this book are incredibly beautiful and thought-provoking. Many people will find comfort in Nancy Stone's words and art, knowing they are not alone."

–Jane Samuelson, director of community relations at Maple Ridge Memory Care

"This poignant and moving collection of haiku by Nancy Stone is a powerful testament to her enduring love, care, and devotion for her husband as she watches his cognitive decline. The title of the book, *Indigo Hours*, evokes a dark blue state of mind. Some poems are surrounded by beautiful drawings depicting the intricate harmony between them and the whimsical lines of the black-and-white background.

I highly recommend this beautiful book of poetry and art to anyone facing similar struggles, or to anyone looking for a deeper understanding of the emotional impact of cognitive decline. This book shows that it is possible through creativity to find moments of beauty and connection even in difficult circumstances.

Nancy's honesty and vulnerability in sharing her experience of what it means to love and care for someone is both touching and inspiring. Her poems offer hope and comfort, not only to others who may be facing similar challenges but for all those who in times of loss find artistic forms of expression."

–*Mina Levinsky-Wohl, LP, LCMHC, psychoanalyst and psychotherapist*

Indigo Hours

Indigo Hours

Healing Haiku

NANCY STONE

Montpelier, VT

Paperback ISBN: 978-1-57869-142-5
Hardcover ISBN: 978-1-57869-143-2
eBook ISBN: 978-1-57869-144-9

Library of Congress Control Number: 2023907734

Published by Rootstock Publishing
an imprint of Ziggy Media LLC
Montpelier, VT 05602 USA

www.rootstockpublishing.com
info@rootstockpublishing.com

Book design by Dana Dwinell-Yardley.
Cover art: "Hourglass" scratchboard art by Nancy Stone.
Author photo by Kate Farrell.

Printed in the USA.

For permissions or to schedule an author interview, contact the author at nstonevt@gmail.com.

To Ken

*For our sixty years of life adventures
that have now quieted to gentle pleasures.*

CONTENTS

Year Four

Year Five

Epilogue

Year One

Future
Entering dense woods
Or the shadowed future
Begins with one step

Meditation

Hearing bird mantra
Healing sun on my cheek
Dawn meditation

Destiny

Our destiny lies
Within the calligraphy
Of a shooting star

Moon
Tidal flow persists
Sleep-starved body resists
While full moon insists

Tremors

Oft times major quakes
Manifest early signs ashore
Less distinct tremors

Clouds

New symptoms appear
Adding to clouds of concern—
Cirrus to Stratus

Worry

Think not, "Thoughts are real"
Reflections on a still pool
Do not hold water!

Patience

Storing patience
Becomes a daily practice
To build up reserves

Panic

Waiting mindfulness
In the calm before the storm
Purgatory pause

Eyes shut, living in
The bubble of not knowing
Until the ears hear...

The hour has arrived
After fear, stress, lost sleep:
CAT scan results come

Dread appears: Brain change!
Panicky attackity
Need a new game plan

Fog

Radiologist

Points us down the primrose path

Heading into fog

*

Our Ben & Jerry's

Pity party lasted 'til

The pint was empty

Loss

Frustration and pain

Abrupt independence loss—

Failed driving test

Ifs

All the 'what ifs'
Have now become the 'when ifs';
Confetti cascade

Heartstrings

Watching from the shore
I see you drifting away
Severing heartstrings

Letters

College love letters
Are memory labyrinths
Leading you to me

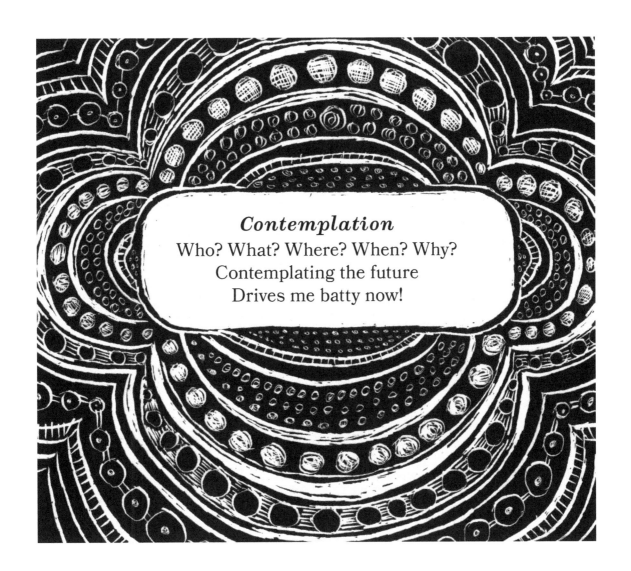

Contemplation

Who? What? Where? When? Why?
Contemplating the future
Drives me batty now!

Forgetting

So many friends
are losing their memories
I forget their names

Vertigo

My own vertigo
Gives me slight insight into
Early dementia

Palimpsest

Writing the present
And future over the past:
Daily palimpsest

Acceptance

Tsunami of fear
Retreats to calm acceptance
Time slows at low tide

Flow

In these later years
Perplexing situations
Do not diminish

Life's changes do not
Imply that 'losses suck' but
Rather, 'rivers flow'

Laughter

Through grieving I learn
Sadness is not depression
Laughing is not wrong

Grief

Grieving recurs as
Wailing harmonica blues
Dark notes search for light

Year Two

Soup

Gourmet cooking skills
Changed to refried bean soup
We eat in silence

Planning

This thinking-for-two
As auxiliary planner
Is a full-time job

Howl

A loud howl woke me
Was it in my dream or did
I hear my own scream?

Co-existence

How can happiness
Co-exist with exhausting
Fear for the future?

Pirates

Though pirates hold maps
With "X" marking the treasure
Our map blew away

Change

At first it's "Oh no!"
Then for awhile it's "Oh well"
At last it's "Of course!"

Foghorn

He touched the wood
Of his well-worn hiking stick
And said, "What is this?"

*

"A man dropped by."
I said, "Could it have been Bert?"
He said, "I don't know."

*

His mind-mist rolls in
I am the foghorn warning
'Stay alert! Take care!'

Nightfall

People ask whether
His memory loss is fast.
How slow is nightfall?

Choice

Betwixt and between
Each day can begin anew....
Choose love and laughter.

Lapses

Am I too alert
To his familiar lapses?
Have they become mine?

Pillow

Through indigo hours
I wander the thought forest
Upon my pillow

Kneading

Making bread or plans
Involves pounding/kneading dough
Or lumpy pillow

Coping

Some days have knives with

Accumulating symptoms

Slicing frequently

At such times I feel

Cracked, crushed and crumpled

Without coping skills

Breathe
When things get tougher
And you are beside yourself
Remember to breathe

Cavities

His daily delight:
Wildlife beyond the window
Our small world expands

Slow excavations
Woodpecker and Alzheimer's
Leaving emptiness

Cavities in trees
Lapses in the brain. Only
The forest resounds

Echoes

His buoyant gladness
Vibrates echoes within
My profound sadness

Kite

Dancing in the breeze
He and the kite are one
Both drift beyond reach

Waves

Waves of symptoms cause
Loss of equilibrium
Roiling out to sea

Don't waste energy
Skipping emotional stones
Across windy waters

Melancholy

Melancholy waves
Flow in strong and linger long
Emotional tides

Quicksand

One saw the other
Flailing within the quicksand
which pulled them both in

Suspension

Suspended in time
We walk the thin curved edge
Of the waning moon

Glance

Buried in my book
I glance up to see his eyes
Eager for some talk

Conversation

This precious time of
Limited conversation
Will drift into mist

Year Three

F-stops

Fiddling with f-stops

In focus; fuzzy focus

Frequent confusion

Crying, "Where are you?"

I see you here yet not there

Our new 'hide and seek'

Hope

Bleak are the colors

Of dementia's tapestry

Rare are Hope's gold threads

Flotsam

Grief's floating flotsam

May linger off-shore...Depends

How the wind doth blow

Obsidian

Molten Tau Tangles

Scour memory, becoming

Hard Obsidian

Geode

Dark crust split open

The geode reveals wondrous

Bright crystals within

Balance

Understand at last
That pleasure and pain in life
Are the Yin and Yang

Midnight

Perhaps it's God's gift
To explore midnight's caverns
The soul's dark canyons

Phoenix

The phoenix ascends
Weaving an ash trail of pale
Memory embers

Elevator

He runs in; I'm left
My panic and he ascend…
Wrong elevator!

Find missing husband:
Baseball cap, White hair, Glasses,
Chocolate addict

Traumatic event
Breaks daily monotony
With anxiety

Dismay

New situation!

Dismay! Search web for answers

Mostly stumbling through

Gait

What is this new sound?

No longer strong foot fall. Now

A shuffling gait

Undertow

Placid days, calm seas
Clandestine tidal movement
Ruthless undertow

Birds

When symptoms rankle
Avert annoyed response.
Reframe your thinking:
Repetition: wren
Thrumming: woodpecker
Social drama: Gull
Mimic: Mockingbird
Complaint growl: Bluejay
Humming: Nightingale
Losing stuff: Raven
Forgetting Who: Owl

Waiting

Watching and waiting
For the next worn shoe to drop
Marking new stumble

Epiphany

Small epiphanies
Amidst cognitive decline
He won at Scrabble!

Tinnitus

Brain Tinnitus:
Tentative intermittent
Wringing of thinking

Tension

Flailing for balance
Either walking or tugging
The cognitive rope

Hiccups

He reacted with
A toddler's pealing laughter
Hiccups while hugging

Searchlight

Through indigo hours
The mind's searchlight spots newly
Unearthed questions

Delight

With a child's delight
He accepts all things as new
Would that I do too!

Walking

From the crack of dawn
Walking the thin liminal
'Til the close of day

Calisthenics

Mind calisthenics
Hither, thither and yon
Wacky sleepless nights

Year Four

Confusion

As was expected
Confusion has arrived
His differs from mine

Uncertain, he asks
"What were we talking about?"
(Up next, "who are you?")

What will it be like
When words no longer engage?
Wind-blown milkweed seed

Shift

Toes at water's edge
Can't hold sand's tidal retreat,
Shifting foundation

Storm

Before the storm: Hope
Within rising waters: "Help"!
After the dark: Heal

Abundance

Embrace abundance

Loss, grief, gladness, hope and love

Life's cup overflows

Gratitude

Unexpectedly

Swelling gratitude rises

Out of grief's dark swale

Release

Release the anguish
Of stumbles in caregiving…
Even the moon rests

Whine

Let the mind have time
To whine: This is getting Old!
ENOUGH ALREADY!

Dawn

In gratitude for
Each dawn leaking hope from dark
The mourning dove sighs

Ambiguity

Here but not really
It comes and goes, highs and lows
Ambiguous grief

Needs

A rising need for
Adult conversations and
Occasional hugs

Anticipation

Not sad so much as
Lonely and disheveled
With loss dipping deep

Losing not only
Long and short memory but
Anticipation

Fulcrum

This/now; that/to come

Balancing on the fulcrum

Daily double-think

Shoulds

The obligations

Tipping points of Life's demands

'Shoulds' now rule my day

Knots

Not liking loose ends
I now feel normal being
All tied up in knots

Dread

After our party
He said, "It was nice being
With those people." (WHAT!!!?)

Was the word not found
Or did he actually
Forget 'family'?!

Weeks of smooth sailing
Interrupted by hull thump
Of submerged dread

Alarm bell ringing
Warning lights blazing brightly
Heart sinks while fears rise

Tangles
Alert at midnight
Thinking meanders wildly
Becoming tangled

Navigation

Such difficult work
Navigating brain's channels
Bleached coral beds

Alchemy

Alchemy is in
This fragile experience
The tincture of time

Dilemma
It's hard trying to
Both hold it together and
Watch it fall apart

Spirit

Fading Life Spirit
Brilliance flows toward soft
Watercolor wash

Dancing

Caregiving involves
More than tending the body…
Dance with the spirit

Year Five

Smörgåsbord

Anxiety. Joy.
Sadness. Regret. Cheerfulness.
Daily smörgåsbord

Solstice

Love is evolving
Sharing becomes caregiving
Our late life solstice

Cocoon

Then, our dreams flew free
Now, our butterfly days
Are shrouded cocoon

Spring

Daffodils. Lilacs.
But will I ever get back
The Spring in my step?

Nautilus

Shells expand for the
Chambered Nautilus. Cells
Shrink from dementia

I'm the one left to
Remember and reminisce
He's just left with Now

Memories

Memories circling
Family photo albums
Rings in Tree of Life

Moments

Tossed and turned
Quiet moments may glow as
Treasured sea glass

Prayer

Pandemics. Droughts. Floods.
Health issues. Politics. War.
The mind needs respite

Equilibrium
Is sought by basking in sun
Eyes shut to the world

But the ears hear new
Reverberations below…
Fracturing ice floe

In darkest of times
Cloak within meditation
Each breath a prayer

Whetstone

Vague thoughts at mid-day
Clarity is sharpened
On midnight's whetstone

Vacation

On vacation, clear
Observation of his dis-
Orientation

The Un-familiar
Causes too much dis-comfort.
Early return home

Cucumber

Small things can break hearts
When asked to fetch "cucumber"
He brought out the grapes

Lotus

Within dark heartbreak
Spirit still sending down roots
Life's Lotus Flower

Time

The full moon questions
Are you truly cherishing
The time remaining?

Hourglass

The pendulum sways
While sand sifts through the hourglass
No time to notice

Now

This is the New Now
Embrace it whole-heartedly
As part of Life's song

Archeology

Grandma told me that
Girls aren't archeologists
Not true nowadays

I'm excavating
Cupboards for lost spoons, pans,
And dirty dishes

An earnest helper
He forgets where things belong
I search and unearth

Icicle

Melting icicle

Weeps bit by bit, drip by drip

As with those who mourn

Heartache day by day

No matter month or season

Accumulation

Eventually

With time, the ice just lets go

Likely tears also

Odyssey

Listen! A soft call—
Snow geese winging on the breeze
Dark lace on bright moon

My spirit seeks to
Join their odyssey from here
To the vast unknown

Train

Bypassing signals
The whistle wails plaintively
"Please. Stop this train NOW!"

But Time hurtles forth
Over trestles of loss, through
Tunnels in the brain

Flickering windows
Reflect precious glimpses of
Shared Memory

Life's receding ties
Diminishing with a whoosh
Soft echoes remain

Today

Despite all the times
Of exasperation, fear,
Exhaustion and stress…

I recognize that
This day could be the Best Day
Of our Yesterdays

Grace

Some mornings glimmer
With gladness and gratitude
Grace notes for the day

Compression

TIGHT compression socks
Frustrating and aggravating
To pull on and off

We shout. I slam door.
He whispers, "I'm sorry for
Whatever I did."

Within just minutes
He forgot what happened
It took me more time

He gently teaches
How to live in the moment
I'm slowly learning

MY HEARTFELT GRATITUDE TO:

Mary Oliver, for her poetry that continues to be a sustaining balm through my years as a caregiver. It sparked my muse to recognize questions while listening for poetic answers.

Dr. Bruce Ross, whose book *Journey to the Interior* celebrates the "experimentation in form" of haiku poetry, diverging from traditional themes of nature to the "exploration of the unfathomable interior of the self."

Friends who insisted that my haiku "must be published." They encouraged me to recognize that my personal quest for understanding held universal themes that could help others. Those advocates are: my Alzheimer's Support Group, my artist support group, the Book Arts Guild of Vermont, Deb Runge, Deb Chisholm, Adrienne Fisher, Kathy Rude, Luba Routsong, and Mina Levinsky-Wohl. Thanks also to friends who patiently listen when conversations are interrupted by my impromptu haiku.

Kate Farrell for her beautiful photographs.

Dana Dwinell-Yardley for the magic she works into book design.

Samantha Kolber for her nurture as poetry editor and publisher of Rootstock Publishing. My journey as a new author could have felt overwhelming. Samantha's expertise and guidance helped me feel empowered.

ABOUT THE AUTHOR

Nancy Stone is an award-winning painter and book artist who taught art at Williston Central School, Vermont Commons School, and Community College of Vermont. Her paintings, mixed media works, and handmade books reflect playful experimentation and imagination. She is a member of the Northern Vermont Artists Association (NVAA) and a Signature Member

of the Vermont Watercolor Society (VWS). She co-founded, and is a member of, the Book Arts Guild of Vermont (BAG). She was art program director of Children's Art Exchange (USA/USSR) and art teacher for Vermont's chapter of Kids4Peace International where she taught Muslim, Christian, and Jewish children from Palestine, Israel, and the USA.

Stone is the author of *251 Vermont Vistas*, a book of her watercolor paintings documenting visits to each of Vermont's 251 towns; the original painted postcards are in the University of Vermont's Special Collection. She and husband Ken were married in 1965; she lives in Williston and he is in memory care. Visit her website to learn more: nancystone.weebly.com.

Rootstock Publishing

More Titles in the Rootstock Poetry Series

Lifting Stones by Doug Stanfield

The Lost Grip by Eva Zimet

Safe as Lightning by Scudder H. Parker

To the Man in the Red Suit by Christina Fulton

Unleashed: Poems & Drawings by Betty Nadine Thomas

Poetry submissions are open now!
Learn more and submit at rootstockpublishing.com.

Printed in the USA
CPSIA information can be obtained
at www.ICGtesting.com
JSHW071448080923
47982JS00006B/12